W9-BNT-263

Let's Find Ads on Signs

by Mari Schuh

first step nonfiction

Lerner Publications ◆ Minneapolis

LERNER

SOURCE

Expand learning beyond the printed book. Download free, complementary educational resources for this book from our website, www.lerneresource.com.

Copyright © 2016 by Lerner Publishing Group, Inc.

All rights reserved. International copyright secured. No part of this book may be reproduced, stored in a retrieval system, or transmitted in any form or by any means—electronic, mechanical, photocopying, recording, or otherwise—without the prior written permission of Lerner Publishing Group, Inc., except for the inclusion of brief quotations in an acknowledged review.

The images in this book are used with the permission of: © Emma Sklar/REX/Newscom, p. 4; © Greg Balfour Evans/Alamy, p. 5; © Zero Creatives/Cultura/Getty Images, p. 6; Method ad via YouTube, p. 7; © Kristoffer Tripplaar/Alamy, p. 8; © Heeb ChristianPrisma Bildagentur AG/Alamy, p. 9; © Mark Sykes/Alamy, p. 10; © BirchTree/Alamy, p. 11; © Patti McConville/Alamy, p. 12; © Stock Connection Blue/Alamy, p. 13; © Richard Levine/Alamy, p. 14; © Joe Vogan/Alamy, p. 15; © Jeff Greenberg 6 of 6/Alamy, p. 16; © Frances M Roberts/Newscom, p. 17; © rSnapshotPhotos/Shutterstock.com, p. 18; © JoeFox/Radharc Images/Alamy, p. 19; © Richard B Levine/Newscom, p. 20; © Nina Prommer/ European Pressphoto Agency/Alamy, p. 21; © Russell Kord/Alamy, p. 22.
Cover: © Findlay/Alamy.

Main body text set in ITC Avant Garde Gothic Std Medium 21/25.
Typeface provided by International Typeface Corp.

Lerner Publications Company
A division of Lerner Publishing Group, Inc.
241 First Avenue North
Minneapolis, MN 55401 USA

For reading levels and more information, look up this title at www.lernerbooks.com.

Library of Congress Cataloging-in-Publication Data

The Cataloging-in-Publication Data for *Let's Find Ads on Signs* is on file at the Library of Congress.
ISBN 978-1-4677-9465-7 (lib. bdg.)
ISBN 978-1-4677-9659-0 (pbk.)
ISBN 978-1-4677-9660-6 (EB pdf)

Manufactured in the United States of America
1 – CG – 12/31/15

Table of Contents

About Ads   4

How Do Signs Work?   10

Where Are Ads on Signs?   14

Thinking about Ads   20

Glossary   23

Index   24

Companies make **products**.

This ad tells about a car.

Presenting the New Toyota
VENZA

Companies use **ads** to tell people about their products.

An ad can make people
want to buy a product.

15 sec by Method Products

method.
CLEAN HAPPY

visit **methodhome.com**

4 PUMPS = 1 LOAD
50 LOADS
BRASSÉES

POWERED BY PLANT-BASED

SMARTCLEAN TECHNOLOGY

method.
8X LAUNDRY
DETERGENT
DÉTERGENT À LESSIVE

FRESH AIR
AIR FRAIS

600mL (20 FL OZ)

0:00 / 1:05:40

)ons for Children Comedy Movies // Animation Movies Full
∇ Kids Movies HD

e Camareno

Subscribe 555

434,205

method.
CLEAN HAPPY   SHOP NOW ⊙

Up Next   Autoplay

Cartoon Movies - The Little Merm
Movie ♥ Little Mermaid Disney

Some ads are videos.

Some ads have words and pictures.

Many companies put ads on signs.

How Do Signs Work?

Signs try to get your **attention**.

Some ads are big and colorful.

Some signs use lights to get your attention.

This ad tells people about a game.

Some signs show videos.

Where Are Ads on Signs?

Companies put ads on signs where many people will see them.

This ad tells people about products that are nearby.

TAKE IT UP A NACHO

GRAB DORITOS® NACHO CHEESE CHIPS WITH YOUR SUB.

When people see an ad for a snack, they might buy the snack.

Many stores show signs with ads on them. People see the ads when they shop.

Some buses have ads.
People read the ad as the
bus goes by.

17

This ad tells people that this house is for sale.

Yards can have signs with ads too.

People who drive by might read this ad.

Some roads have big signs with ads. These ads are called **billboards**.

19

Thinking about Ads

Ads ask people to take action.

These ads ask people to see a movie.

What does this ad ask you to do?